My Cool Sister

By Gail Kimberly

Illustrated by Elizabeth Sawyer

DOMINIE PRESS

Pearson Learning Group

Publisher: Raymond Yuen
Project Editor: John S. F. Graham
Editor: Bob Rowland
Designer: Greg DiGenti
Illustrator: Elizabeth Sawyer

Published by:

🦷 **Dominie Press, Inc.**

1949 Kellogg Avenue
Carlsbad, California 92008 USA

www.dominie.com

1-800-232-4570

Paperback ISBN 0-7685-2075-4
Printed in Singapore by PH Productions Pte Ltd
4 5 6 PH 05

Table of Contents

Chapter One
My Big Sister, Caitlin

My big sister, Caitlin, is really cool. She can play the piano and the flute. She can beat anybody at video games. She glued the wheel back on my toy truck when it fell off. She even taught our little Scottie dog, Fang, to catch Frisbees.

Caitlin's eleven, and most of the time she hangs out with her girlfriends. She hardly ever plays with me. She says that's because I'm a boy, but I think it's because I'm not cool, like her and her friends. It's hard to be cool when you're only seven.

But when we went to stay with Grandpa for awhile last summer, Caitlin only had me and Fang to hang out with.

Grandpa lives on a farm with a lot of horses and chickens, but no kids. He lets us ride the horses sometimes when he goes with us. One time he took us fishing down at the lake. Sometimes he plays baseball in the yard with us, too, but most of the time he's too busy.

So Caitlin and I were batting balls to each other that afternoon when Fang somehow got outside the fence and

ran away. I should have been watching him more closely. I knew the fence wasn't in great shape, but Fang had never run away before.

We didn't notice he was gone until it was nearly time for dinner. Then Caitlin said we should go inside and help set the table. But Fang didn't come when we called him. I even whistled for him. Fang always comes when you whistle.

Chapter Two
We Have to Go Farther

"**W**e should go and look for him,"
I said, "but Grandpa told us to stay here
in the yard."

"Oh, Brian, Grandpa won't mind,"
Caitlin said. "Fang's lost. We have to
find him. Then we'll come right back.

We won't be long."

"OK," I said and followed her through the gate.

"Fang probably saw a rabbit and chased it," Caitlin said.

"Or maybe a squirrel," I said. "Squirrels live in trees. Look at all those trees."

There was a forest behind the house. So that's where we went.

It was dark in the forest. The trees were so close together that their branches blocked the sky. Old logs were lying on the ground with moss all over them. There were some empty cans, too, and pieces of plastic and cardboard.

"People shouldn't throw all of that on the ground," I said. "They should use garbage cans."

Caitlin called out, "Fang! Come here."

We waited. I saw birds in the trees.

I saw some little blue flowers. I saw a caterpillar on a bush. But I didn't see Fang.

"We have to go farther," Caitlin said.

"But we could get lost," I said. "Like Hansel and Gretel. Remember the story? We should have brought crumbs to throw on the ground and make a trail. Then we could follow it back to Grandpa's."

"Don't be silly," Caitlin said. "In the story, the birds ate the crumbs. They'd eat ours, too. We don't need a crumb trail. I can find the way back."

"OK," I said.

Chapter Three
Which Way Is Home?

We walked a long way, stepping over more moss-covered logs and empty cans. I couldn't see very far ahead because of all the trees and thick bushes.

"Do you think there are bears here?" I asked Caitlin.

"Bears?" Caitlin stopped and looked at me. Her eyes were very big. "Don't say things like that, Brian. You're just going to scare me."

"Don't be scared," I told her. "If Fang saw a bear, he'd bark and we'd hear him."

And then, just as if he were listening, we heard Fang barking. He wasn't very far away.

"That's Fang!" Caitlin shouted. "Come on, Brian. Let's go get him."

"But maybe he's barking at a bear," I said. "We'd better just stay here and call him. We can hear him, so he must be able to hear us."

We called as loudly as we could, and I whistled. In a minute we heard leaves rustling and then the sound of Fang panting and scrambling over the logs.

Pretty soon he found us. He was glad

to see us. He jumped on our legs and
wagged his tail so hard, he nearly fell over.

"You made us late for dinner," I told
him. "I hope Grandpa won't be worried."

"Come on," Caitlin said. "Let's go
home."

"Which way is home?" I asked her.

Caitlin looked around, "Ummm..."

Chapter Four
I Think It's This Way

The trees and bushes around us all looked the same. There were moss-covered logs here, too, and empty cans. It was just like everyplace else in the forest.

Caitlin looked puzzled. Then she

pointed. "I think it's this way," she said.

"OK," I said. I followed her, and Fang followed both of us.

We walked for a long time. We walked between trees and over more moss-covered logs. We saw more empty cans and one green sock somebody must have dropped.

"I don't remember that green sock," I said.

Then Caitlin stopped. "I don't think this is the right way," she said. "Maybe it's that way." She pointed back the way we had come.

"OK," I said. "Let's try it."

We walked and walked. It was getting dark, and we didn't have a flashlight. The moon shone between the trees, and I could see more and more stars as we walked.

Caitlin stopped again and leaned against a tree trunk. "I think we're lost, Brian."

"I think you're right," I said.

"We can't just keep walking around," Caitlin said.

"Maybe we should wait here," I told her. "When we're not back for dinner, Grandpa will look for us. He might find us."

"But he doesn't know we came into the forest," Caitlin said. "He won't know where to look."

I looked at the tree she was leaning on. It had wide, low branches near the bottom, and it was very tall. I got an idea.

Chapter Five
Follow Me, Guys

"**D**o you remember the big bright light on the post in front of Grandpa's house?" I asked Caitlin.

"The one that goes on at night? Of course I do," she said.

"Do you think it's bright enough so

you can see it from far away?" I asked.

"Yes," she said. "It is. But we can't see it here. The trees are in the way."

"I could climb one of the trees," I said. "If I can see Grandpa's light from the top of the tree, we'll know which way to go."

"Hey, that's a good idea, Brian," Caitlin said. She sounded surprised.

I looked around to see which tree would be the best one to climb.

"I'll try that one." I pointed to one with wide, low branches.

"That's not a very tall one," Caitlin said. "Shouldn't you find a taller one?"

"This is the one that looks the easiest to climb," I said. "We should think about being safe."

I looked up into the tree from below. The branches made almost a perfect ladder that went straight up. But the first branch was too high for me. I tried to pull myself up to it from the trunk, but it was still too high. I couldn't reach it.

"I'll help you," Caitlin said. She jumped up and grabbed the branch, hanging on to it with both hands.

The branch bent down far enough so that I could reach it from the ground.

"Now try it," she said.

I pulled myself up onto it with my arms, and then I got one leg over. I moved along the branch to the trunk.

"You can let go!" I called down to Caitlin.

The next branch up was just above me, so it was easy for me to climb onto that one. Pretty soon I was high up in the tree. I looked around.

"I can see Grandpa's light!" I shouted. "It's over there."

I pointed to it, but I don't think she could see me. It was too dark.

"Just remember which direction it is," she yelled back. When I climbed down the tree, I knew which way we should go.

"It's that way," I said, pointing.

"That's great," Caitlin said with a big smile. She sounded different. She sounded like she was proud of me. "Follow me, guys," she said.

"OK," I said.

Fang was wagging his tail, and I was happy, too. It's no fun to be lost in the dark woods.

When we got back to Grandpa's house he was so glad to see us, he forgot to be angry that we left without telling anyone.

We told him everything that had happened.

"And then we got lost," Caitlin said.

Grandpa smiled. "It wasn't very smart to let Fang get away," he said. "But you were both very smart to find him and then find your way home again in the dark."

"Brian was the one who remembered your light, Grandpa," Caitlin said. "And he was the one who climbed that tree to see where it was."

Then she gave me a big hug. "My little brother is so cool!" she told Grandpa.